D1540785

WORLD BOOK'S
YOUNG SCIENTIST

WORLD BOOK'S

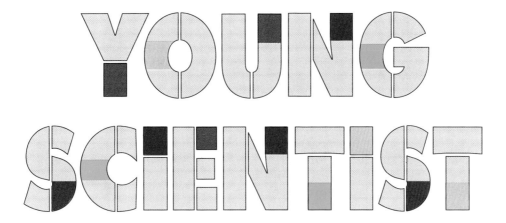

Space Technology

World Book, Inc.
a Scott Fetzer company
Chicago London Sydney Toronto

Activities that have this warning symbol require some adult supervision!

The quest to explore the known world and to describe its creation and subsequent development is nearly as old as mankind. In the Western world, the best-known creation story comes from the book of Genesis. It tells how God created the earth and all living things. Modern religious thinkers interpret the Biblical story of creation in various ways. Some believe that creation occurred exactly as Genesis describes it. Others think that God's method of creation is revealed through scientific investigation. *Young Scientist* presents an exciting picture of what scientists have learned about life and the universe.

World Book, Inc.
525 W. Monroe
Chicago, IL 60661

For information on other World Book products, call 1-800-255-1750.

ISBN: 0-7166-6309-0
Library of Congress Catalog Card No. 95-61305

Printed in Mexico

1 2 3 4 5 6 7 8 9 10 99 98 97 96 95

Acknowledgments

The publishers of **World Book's Young Scientist** acknowledge the following photographers, publishers, agencies, and corporations for photographs used in this volume.

Cover	Tony Craddock, Dr. Seth Shostak (Science Photo Library)
8/9	Hank Morgan (Science Photo Library); Spectrum Colour Library; ZEFA Picture Library
12/13	Sarah Errington (Hutchison Library)
18/19	Phil Jude (Science Photo Library)
24/25	Tim Defrisc (Allsport Photographic)
28/29	David Higgs (Tony Stone Worldwide)
30/31	Peter Aitken (Science Photo Library)
32/33	Nelson Morris (Science Photo Library)
54/55	ZEFA Picture Library; Tony Stone Worldwide
56/57	Tom Sheppard (Tony Stone Worldwide)
58/59	ZEFA Picture Library

Illustrated by

Hemesh Alles
Sue Barclay
Richard Berridge
Bristol Illustrators
Marie DeJohn
Farley, White and Veal
Peter Geissler
Jeremy Gower
Kathie Kelleher
John Lobban
Louise Martin
Jeremy Pyke
Don Simpson
Gary Slater
Pat Tourret
Peter Visscher
Matthew White
Lynne Willey

Contents

Journey into space

In ancient times, astronomers studied the stars in the night sky. Later, they were able to gaze through telescopes. Today, we can study space from space itself. Astronomers have discovered all kinds of remarkable things about space from satellites and other spacecraft that journey to the **planets.** Planets are heavenly bodies which travel around a sun.

We live at the bottom of a thick layer of gases called the **atmosphere.** This provides us with oxygen to breathe, it keeps us warm, and it protects us. As we travel up through the earth's atmosphere, the gases are less concentrated. As the air becomes thinner and thinner, it grows difficult to breathe. At a height of about 6 miles (10 kilometers), we can't breathe at all without extra oxygen. Higher still, only a whiff of air remains. When we reach a height of 99 miles (160 kilometers), there is almost no air at all. We are about to enter space.

What is space?

In space there is no atmosphere. So sound cannot travel and there is no weather as we know it on earth. Space is full of dangerous rays and particles traveling at high speed. Space begins where the earth's atmosphere has faded to almost nothing. We do not know where space ends. Spacecraft have traveled from earth to the most distant planets of our solar system. But the stars that lie in deep space have never been explored. They are millions and millions of miles beyond our solar system.

These rockets are examples of the types of rockets that have sent spacecraft or satellites into space. You can see them at the Visitors' Center at Cape Canaveral, Florida.

The daytime sky

Every morning the sun rises, bringing light and warmth to our world. It is daytime. The sun rises in the east, and during the day it appears to travel in an arc across the sky. In the evening, it sets in the west. As it disappears below the horizon, the earth becomes dark. It is night.

However, this is not really what happens. The sun only seems to move across the sky. It is the earth, not the sun, that is moving. The earth is spinning in space. The sun moves into our view and out of sight again as the earth whirls around. It takes the earth 24 hours to turn around an imaginary line that runs from the North Pole to the South Pole. We call this line the earth's **axis.**

Without the sun's light and heat, the earth would be a dark, cold world. Plants need sunlight to make their food. Animals cannot make their own food. They must eat plants or other animals in order to live. So without sunlight, there would be no living things.

The earth turns on its axis once every 24 hours.

What is the sun?

The sun is a star and is similar to the other stars in the sky. It appears bigger and brighter because it is much nearer than other stars. It lies about 93 million miles (150 million kilometers) away. The star nearest to us after the sun is over 25 million million miles (40 million million kilometers) away! Heat from the sun warms the earth. The highest temperature recorded on earth was 136 °F (58 °C). The temperature near the surface of the sun is 10,000 °F (5500 °C)! At the sun's center, the temperature rises to about 27,000,000 °F (15,000,000 °C).

Sometimes we can see dark patches on the surface of the sun. These are called **sunspots.** We may also see arcs of gas called **prominences** or bursts of light called **flares.** Prominences and flares are types of solar storms. They usually happen above sunspots.

You will need:

sheets of cardboard

a compass

a piece of string

a thumbtack

a pencil

a ruler

Scaling the sun

This experiment shows the earth and the sun to scale in size and distance.

1. On a small sheet of cardboard, use a compass to draw a circle about 3/16 inch (4 millimeters) across. This represents the earth.

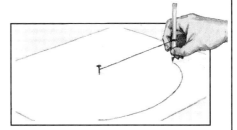

2. On a large sheet of cardboard draw a circle 17 9/16 inches (44 centimeters) across. Do this by tying a pencil to a piece of string. Pin the other end of the string to the middle of the cardboard 8 3/4 inches (22 centimeters) away from the pencil.

3. Take 100 large steps to measure out a distance of about 165 feet (50 meters), and mark the place. Keep the earth card yourself, and ask a friend to take the sun card and stand at the 165-foot (50-meter) mark.

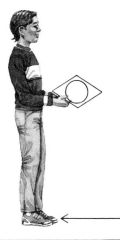

←——————165 feet (50 meters)——————→

Find out more by looking at
pages **30–31**
         56–57

The moon

On most nights of the year, the sky is lit up by our nearest neighbor in space, the moon. The Latin word for the moon is *luna*. The word **lunar** means anything to do with the moon. The moon travels around the earth in just over 27 days.

Have you noticed that the moon seems to change shape as the month goes by? The moon does not give out its own light, but we can see it because it reflects sunlight. It also moves around the sun and, as it does, the sun's light falls on part of its surface. The shape we see depends on how much of the moon's surface that faces us is lit up by the sun. The changing shapes are called **phases.**

The moon has a much weaker **gravity,** or pull, than the earth. Because of this, it cannot hold on to any gases to make up an atmosphere. Where there is no atmosphere, there can be no sound and no weather.

In this diagram, the sun and moon are shown much closer to the earth than they really are.

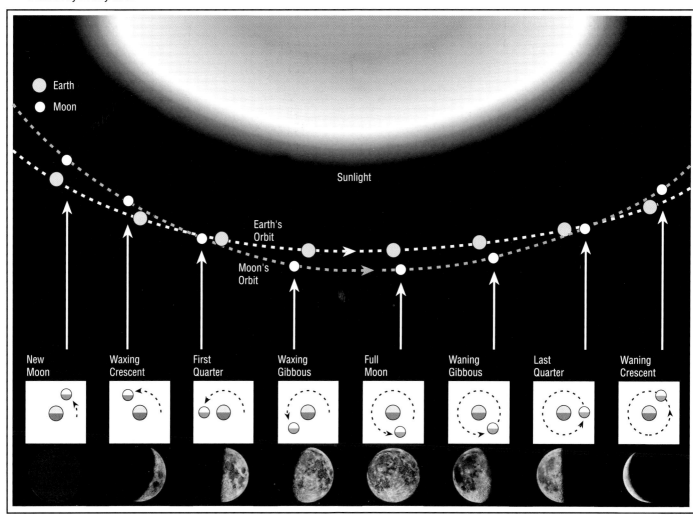

This is the side of the moon that we can see from earth. Highlands cover most of the far side of the moon.

The moon's phases

The moon's phases are caused by the position of the moon in relation to the sun and earth. When the moon is between the earth and the sun, we can't see it at all. We call it the *new moon*. About a week later, we see half of it lit up. This is the *first quarter*. About a week later, all of it is lit up and it is the *full moon*. It is half lit up again at the last quarter, about a week later. It eventually disappears at the next new moon, 29½ days after the previous one.

As the moon changes from new moon to full moon, it is said to be *waxing*. During the period from full moon back to new moon, it is said to be *waning*. When the moon looks larger than half a full moon, it is called *gibbous*.

The moon's dimensions

Part of the surface of the moon consists of great, flat plains that are covered in dust. The rest of the surface is made up of highlands and towering mountain ranges. Some of the mountains soar to a height of over 23,100 feet (7,000 meters).

Everywhere on the surface there are **craters,** which are holes made by lumps of rock raining down from outer space. The smaller craters are just a few inches wide, while others are great depressions or pits up to 700 miles (1,100 kilometers) across.

The moon is about a quarter the size of the earth. It measures 2,160 miles (3,476 kilometers) across. The distance from the earth to the moon is about 238,857 miles (384,403 kilometers). We never see the far side of the moon from earth. This is because the moon rotates on its axis in the same time it takes to circle the earth. But we know what the far side of the moon looks like from photographs taken by satellites in space or by astronauts in their spacecraft.

Find out more by looking at
pages 16–17
           18–19

The starry heavens

Look up at the sky on a clear, moonless night and you will see thousands of stars twinkling in a black, velvety sky.

If you gaze for a while, you will notice that some of the bright stars could be joined up to make patterns in the sky. These patterns of stars are called **constellations.** Ancient stargazers gave the constellations names that somewhat fit their shapes. We still use many of these names today.

People living north of the equator can easily recognize the **Big Dipper.** It is shaped like a long-handled cup, or dipper. It is part of the constellation of the Great Bear, or Ursa Major. Nearby is Ursa Minor, or the Little Bear. The brightest star in Ursa Minor is the **North Star,** also called the polestar. People living south of the equator may be able to find the Southern Cross. This lies near one of the brightest groups of stars in the southern sky, Alpha Centauri.

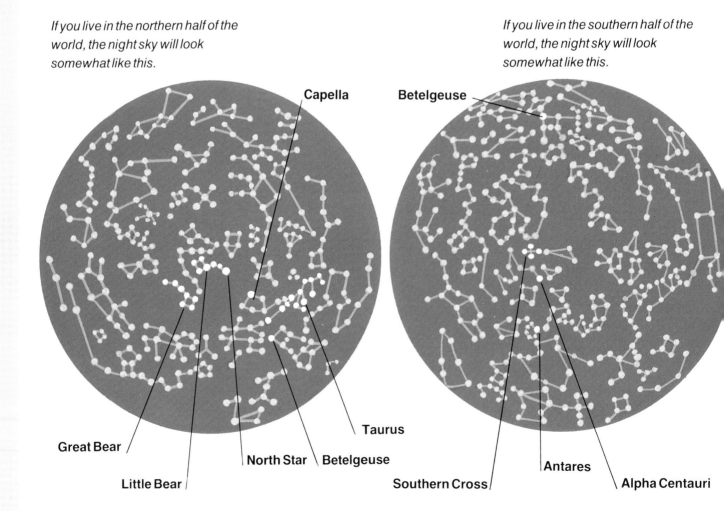

If you live in the northern half of the world, the night sky will look somewhat like this.

If you live in the southern half of the world, the night sky will look somewhat like this.

Capella

Betelgeuse

Taurus

Great Bear

North Star   Betelgeuse

Little Bear

Southern Cross

Antares

Alpha Centauri

Make a star viewer

You will need:

a cardboard box

scissors

a cardboard tube

black poster paint

aluminum foil

black cotton thread

adhesive tape

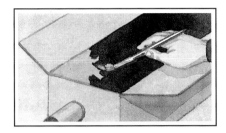

1. Cut a hole in the end of your box, large enough to push the cardboard tube about 1 inch (2.5 centimeters) into the box. Paint the inside of your box black. Cut off the two end flaps.

2. Cut different lengths of thread. Tie a knot at the end of each one. Wrap some aluminum foil around each knot to form a ball. Attach the other end of one thread to the top of the box with adhesive tape. Hang the rest of the foil balls in a row inside the box.

3. Fold long flaps of the box together and loosely tape them shut. Now look through the tube. All the silver balls seem to be grouped together because it is black all around them.

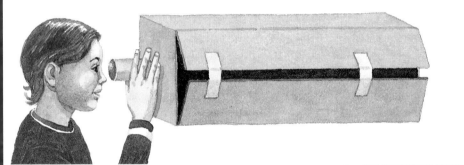

Clustering together

The stars in the constellations are not really grouped together in space. They only appear to be close because they happen to lie in the same direction. But sometimes, thousands and thousands of stars crowd together in ball-like groups called **globular clusters.**

Other clusters, called **open clusters,** contain between ten and a few hundred stars and have an irregular shape. We can see one open cluster without a telescope. It is in the constellation of Taurus. This cluster is called the Pleiades, or Seven Sisters. People with good eyesight may be able to see its six brightest stars.

The sun is quite a small star. We call it a dwarf. Many stars are considerably larger. Antares is so big we call it a supergiant. And Betelgeuse is even bigger, hundreds of times bigger than the sun.

A star is born ...

Throughout the universe, there are great clouds of gas and dust. These clouds are called **nebulae.** In larger nebulae, stars may form. The process begins when gravity pulls the gas and dust particles together. As the mass of particles becomes tightly packed, or compressed, it heats up. In time, the temperature inside rises to about 2,000,000 °F (1,100,000 °C).

At such temperatures, atoms of hydrogen gas begin to combine, or fuse, together to form helium gas. As they do so, they release an enormous amount of energy as light and heat. The mass of gas and dust begins to shine—as a star.

... and dies

A star the size of the sun has a long life. The sun is now about 4.6 billion years old and will probably stay as it is for another 5 billion years. Then, scientists believe, it will run out of hydrogen "fuel" and begin to die. First, it will swell in size and become a type of star we call a **red giant.** Then it will slowly shrink again, becoming smaller and smaller, until it is not much bigger than the earth. It will become a body called a **white dwarf.** For their size, white dwarfs are very heavy. A teaspoonful of material from a white dwarf weighs many tons!

The heavyweights

Big, heavy stars die spectacular deaths. They swell up into enormous supergiants, many times their own size. Then, they blast themselves apart in a mighty explosion called a **supernova.**

After a supernova, a tiny star sometimes remains. It is called a **neutron star,** because it is made up of tiny particles called neutrons. Very heavy stars do not form neutron stars. They continue collapsing under gravity until they crush themselves into a very small space. All that remains is a small area with an enormous gravity. This swallows up anything nearby, even light. For this reason we call it a **black hole.**

1

6

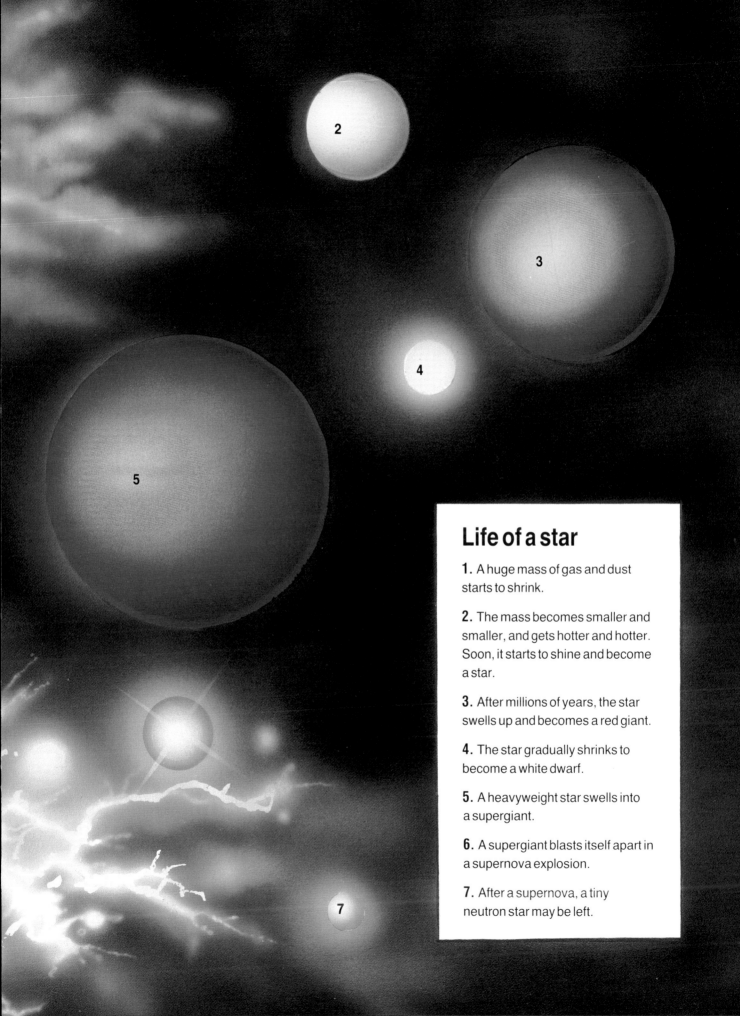

Life of a star

1. A huge mass of gas and dust starts to shrink.

2. The mass becomes smaller and smaller, and gets hotter and hotter. Soon, it starts to shine and become a star.

3. After millions of years, the star swells up and becomes a red giant.

4. The star gradually shrinks to become a white dwarf.

5. A heavyweight star swells into a supergiant.

6. A supergiant blasts itself apart in a supernova explosion.

7. After a supernova, a tiny neutron star may be left.

Star islands

If you look up at the heavens on a very dark night, you might see a fuzzy band of light across the sky. This is a band of stars called the **Milky Way.**

These stars, and most of the others we can see, belong to a great island of stars spinning through space. This island is the **Milky Way Galaxy.** The earth is in this galaxy. Scientists believe that the Milky Way Galaxy is just one of millions of galaxies in the universe. It is shaped like a disk with a bulge in the middle. The stars are arranged in groups like curving arms that spiral out from the center.

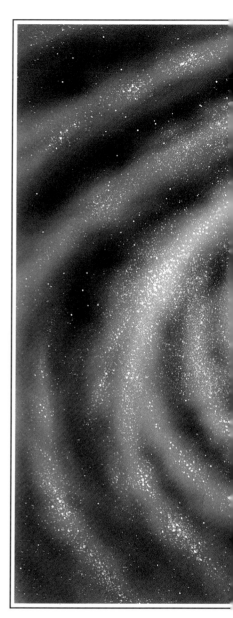

Expand the universe

You will need:

a large round balloon

a black pen

1. Partly blow up the balloon.

2. With your pen, draw large spots all over it roughly the same distance apart.

3. Continue blowing up the balloon until it is much bigger. Notice how all the spots have moved away from each other.

 Imagine the skin of the balloon is the universe, and the spots are the galaxies. By blowing up the balloon and making the spots move farther apart, you can parallel what most scientists believe is happening in space. The universe is expanding, with all the galaxies rushing away from one another.

Our own galaxy would look something like this if we could see it floating in space. It is so big that it would take 100,000 years for a light beam to travel from one side to the other! The sun is one of hundreds of thousands of millions of stars in the Milky Way Galaxy.

The outer galaxies

There are many other galaxies shaped like ours. We call them **spiral** galaxies. Some galaxies are round or oval. These are called **elliptical** galaxies. Others have no regular shape.

Most galaxies are so far away that we cannot see them without a telescope. But we can see a few. Two can be seen as white patches by people south of the equator. They are called the Small and Large Magellanic Clouds. People north of the equator can see another, in the constellation Andromeda. The Andromeda Galaxy is the nearest of the great spiral galaxies.

Find out more by looking at
pages **22–23**
24–25

The solar system

The earth spins around on its axis once a day. The earth also moves in another way. It travels in an elliptical, or oval-shaped, **orbit** around the sun. It takes just over 365 days to make the journey. This is the period we call a year.

The earth is not the only large body to circle the sun. There are eight others, which we call **planets.** Each planet circles the sun at a different distance and takes a different amount of time to complete its orbit. In order, starting nearest the sun, the planets are Mercury, Venus, Earth, Mars, Jupiter, Saturn, Uranus, Neptune, and Pluto. These planets form the main part of the sun's family, or the **solar system.**

The solar system also includes many other smaller bodies. Several of the planets are themselves the center of miniature systems with many satellites, or moons, circling around them. There is another group of large, rocky bodies called **asteroids.** They circle in a broad band, or belt, between the orbits of Mars and Jupiter. The sun's family also includes **comets** and **meteors,** or shooting stars, which are the smaller streaks of light we see in the night sky.

Mercury, Venus, and Mars are often called the terrestrial planets. This is because they are small, rocky planets, like Earth.

Sun

Mercury

Venus

Earth

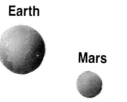

Mars

Jupiter

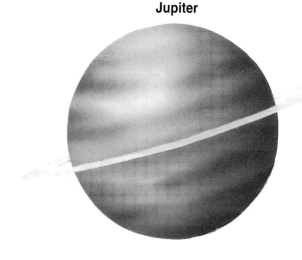

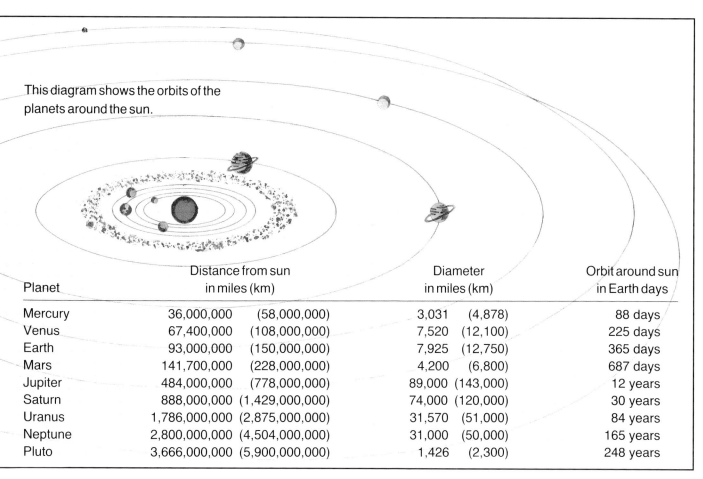

This diagram shows the orbits of the planets around the sun.

Planet	Distance from sun in miles (km)		Diameter in miles (km)		Orbit around sun in Earth days
Mercury	36,000,000	(58,000,000)	3,031	(4,878)	88 days
Venus	67,400,000	(108,000,000)	7,520	(12,100)	225 days
Earth	93,000,000	(150,000,000)	7,925	(12,750)	365 days
Mars	141,700,000	(228,000,000)	4,200	(6,800)	687 days
Jupiter	484,000,000	(778,000,000)	89,000	(143,000)	12 years
Saturn	888,000,000	(1,429,000,000)	74,000	(120,000)	30 years
Uranus	1,786,000,000	(2,875,000,000)	31,570	(51,000)	84 years
Neptune	2,800,000,000	(4,504,000,000)	31,000	(50,000)	165 years
Pluto	3,666,000,000	(5,900,000,000)	1,426	(2,300)	248 years

Jupiter, Saturn, Uranus, and Neptune are often called the giant planets. They are made mainly of gases. It is believed that Pluto is mainly icy.

Pluto

Neptune

Uranus

Saturn

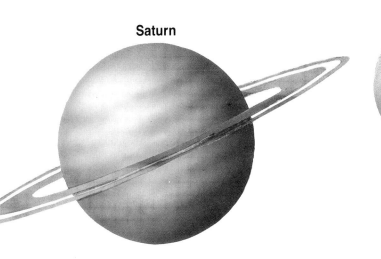

Find out more by looking at pages **20–21**

The planets

From the earth, we can see six of the other planets in our solar system without a telescope. They look like bright stars, but they change their position from night to night. This is why they are called *planets. Planet* means "wanderer."

The six planets are Mercury, Venus, Mars, Jupiter, Saturn, and Uranus. We can see them because they reflect the light of the sun—just as our moon does. The planet closest to us, Venus, is also the brightest. We see Venus sometimes at dawn as the "morning star" and sometimes at sunset as the "evening star." When they are closest to Earth, Mars and Jupiter shine nearly as brightly as Venus. Mars is easy to spot because it has a reddish-orange color. It is often called the Red Planet.

You can see Jupiter's four largest moons through an ordinary telescope. A Voyager spacecraft took these pictures of them.

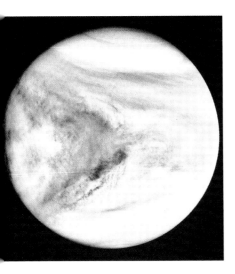

Venus is a terrestrial planet made of rock. It is one of our nearest neighbors.

The bright planets

Mars and Venus appear so bright because they are our nearest neighbors among the planets. Jupiter lies very far away. It seems bright because it is so gigantic. It is more than a thousand times bigger than Earth! In fact, it is the biggest planet in the solar system.

What are they made of ?

Mars, Venus, and Mercury are balls of rock, like Earth. They are often called the **terrestrial,** or Earthlike, planets. The four giant planets—Jupiter, Saturn, Uranus, and Neptune—consist mainly of gas. These planets are similar in other ways. They are surrounded by **rings** made up of pieces of rock and ice. And they are at the center of miniature systems made up of many satellites, or moons.

Odd one out

The odd planet out is Pluto. This is the smallest planet of all, but it is so far away that we know little about it. It was not even discovered until 1930. It is a frozen world, with temperatures believed to be around $-355\,°F$ $(-215\,°C)$. Pluto has a moon called Charon.

Saturn has at least 18 moons. It is surrounded by rings of rock and ice.

Rocky bits and pieces

Scientists think that the planets were made from material that was left over from the gas cloud that formed the sun. After the planets and their moons were made, many more pieces of material remained. These pieces are still there, hurtling around the sun in their own orbits, like miniature planets. The biggest group of pieces is the **asteroids.** They circle in a broad "belt" between Mars and Jupiter. There are thousands of these rocky lumps. The biggest, called Ceres, is almost 620 miles (1,000 kilometers) across. But most are very much smaller.

Shooting stars

Have you ever seen what looks like a star falling from the heavens? You can see it happening on most clear nights, when streaks of white fire appear in the sky. Some people call these streaks "shooting stars." But the stars are not really falling, of course. What you see are tiny pieces of rock from outer space — some as small as grains of sand — hurtling through the upper air. The rubbing, or **friction,** of the air makes the pieces heat up and glow. Most of them quickly burn up and turn to dust.

The proper name for these shooting stars is **meteors.** The pieces that do not burn up completely, before falling to the ground, are called **meteorites.** Large meteorites can make huge craters when they hit the ground.

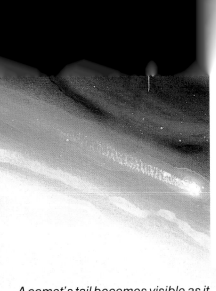

Comets

Other wandering lumps of ice and dust can sometimes put on a really spectacular show in the night sky. They are called **comets.** They have a large, glowing head and a tail of gas and dust that can stretch far across the sky.

A comet's tail becomes visible as it nears the sun. Particles streaming from the sun blow some of the comet's gas and dust into a tail. The tail always points away from the sun.

A huge lump of rock from outer space made this vast crater in the state of Arizona about 50,000 years ago. It measures about 4,150 feet (1,265 meters across and is about 570 feet (174 meters) deep.

Light telescopes

Our eyes are good enough for simple stargazing. But they tell us very little about the stars. To see the stars more clearly, we need to look through a **telescope.** The word *telescope* means "far-seeing," and that is just what a telescope enables us to do.

Refracting and reflecting telescopes

In 1609, the Italian scientist Galileo Galilei became the first person to study the heavens through a telescope. Galileo's telescope used glass lenses. Some astronomers still use this type of telescope today. It is called a **refracting** telescope because the lenses refract, or bend, light into the observer's eye. But the biggest and most powerful telescopes use mirrors to gather starlight. They are called **reflecting** telescopes because the mirrors reflect light into the eye.

You will need:

three sheets of paper

tape

a desk lamp

a pen or pencil

Why is bigger better?

Here's a simple activity that demonstrates how bigger lenses capture more light.

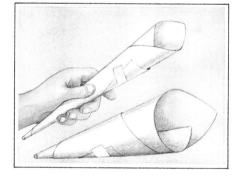

1. Roll one sheet of paper into a cone with the small opening slightly larger across than a pencil lead and the large opening 2 to 3 inches (5 to 7.5 centimeters) across. Tape the ends in place.

2. Roll and tape the second paper into a cone with the small opening the same size and the large opening at least 4 1/2 inches (11.25 centimeters) across.

3. Turn on the desk lamp and place the third piece of paper on the table under it, as shown.

4. Hold the first sheet of paper under the lamp with the large end toward the lamp. Adjust the distance to the paper so that a small, sharp circle of light falls on the paper.

This big reflecting telescope can swivel and turn. The telescope can be pointed in any direction. Several different mirrors produce an image in different places. It is so big that an astronomer can sit inside the telescope tube!

5. Start moving the cone sideways out of the light until the dot fades.

6. With your pencil, mark the spot where the dot of light disappears.

7. Repeat steps 4, 5, and 6 with the larger cone. Make sure you're holding the small end of the cone the same distance from the paper as you did in step 4. What do you notice?

The larger cone collects more light, so the spot on the paper is brighter. You also can move it farther away from the source of light and still get an image. Similarly, large telescopes can produce images of dimmer, more distant stars better than smaller ones can.

Big telescopes

The telescopes professional astronomers use are far bigger than the kind you can buy to use at home. That's because the bigger the lenses, the more light the telescope can collect. The Bolshoi Teleskop Aximutal'ny in Russia, for example, is 19 1/4 feet (6 meters) across. The Keck Telescope in Hawaii is even bigger—33 feet (10 meters) across. This light-collecting power enables astronomers to study distant objects in the universe.

Find out more by looking at pages **16–17**

Other telescopes

Stars give out energy in many forms. Light is just one of them. Stars also give out **radio waves,** which travel well through the earth's atmosphere. Astronomers study these waves with radio telescopes. **Radio telescopes** use bowl-shaped reflectors to gather the radio signals and focus them on to an antenna. Using a computer, scientists convert the signals into a picture. Radio pictures of stars and galaxies are often different from photographs taken with light.

Stars also give out, or radiate, energy as **ultraviolet rays** and **infrared rays.** Ultraviolet rays in sunlight are the ones that darken fair skin and can cause sunburn. Infrared rays carry heat. Scientists cannot easily study the infrared and ultraviolet rays from the stars. This is because the earth's atmosphere stops most of this radiation from reaching their telescopes.

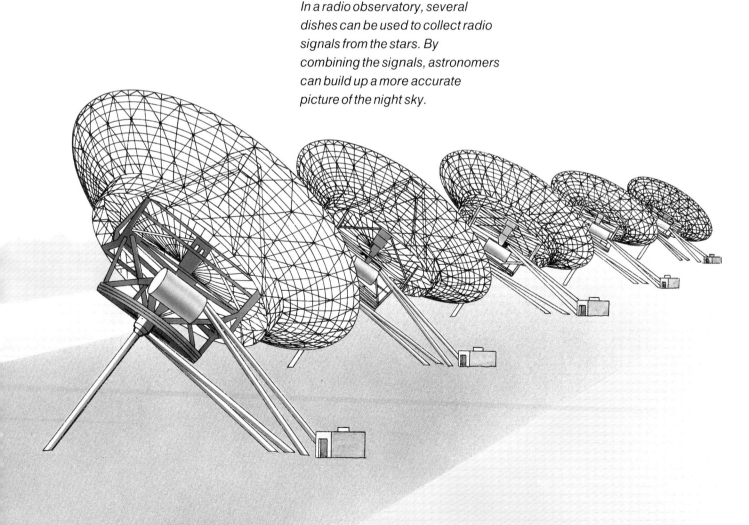

In a radio observatory, several dishes can be used to collect radio signals from the stars. By combining the signals, astronomers can build up a more accurate picture of the night sky.

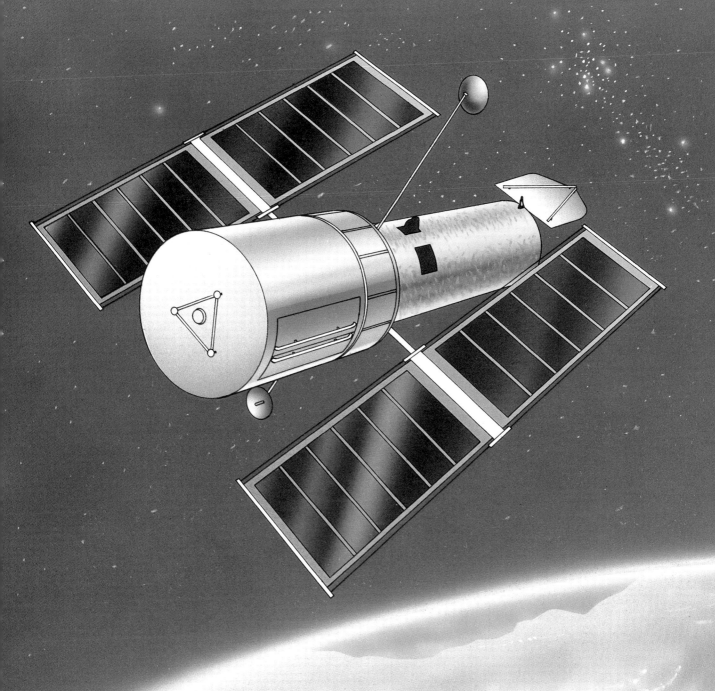

Telescopes in space

Space is a good place to study astronomy. There is nothing, not even air, in space to stop us from collecting the different rays the stars give out. So astronomers send telescopes into space. These telescopes measure ultraviolet, infrared, and X rays coming from outer space. We have made many interesting discoveries using these telescopes. We have seen stars being born, discovered new comets, and found places where there may be those mysterious black holes.

The Hubble space telescope is a reflecting telescope. It is sensitive to visible and ultraviolet light from stars. It has a mirror nearly 9 feet (2.5 meters) across. In orbit, it can detect light many times farther into space than we can from the earth.

Find out more by looking at pages **12–13**

The laws of space

What happens when you jump up into the air? Do you continue moving upwards? Of course not. You soon come down to the ground again. Why? Because the earth is pulling you down. The force which pulls us towards the earth is called gravity. Gravity makes everything that you drop fall. On earth, it holds everything in place—rocks, trees, buildings, seas, and even the air.

Matter has gravity. The bigger a lump of matter is, the greater is its gravity. The moon is much smaller than earth and has a much lower gravity—only one-sixth of the earth's gravity. So if your weight is 132 pounds (60 kilograms) on earth, it would be 22 pounds (10 kilograms) on the moon. Jupiter has a much stronger gravity because it is much bigger than the earth.

The sun has an enormous field of gravity, which stretches for thousands of millions of miles. It keeps the planets orbiting around the sun.

Get set for the interplanetary high jump! If you are a good high-jumper on earth, you may clear 3 feet (almost 1 meter). On the moon, which has low gravity, you will clear 20 feet (6 meters). On Jupiter, which has high gravity, you will clear only about 14 inches (35 centimeters)!

Light and distance

Suppose that you live 1 mile (1.6 kilometers) from school and that it takes 15 minutes to walk there. If someone asked you how far it is to school, you could say "15 minutes." You could use time to measure the distance from home to school.

Astronomers measure distance in units of time. But the distances between planets and stars are huge. So we use a special unit called a **light-year.** One light-year equals 5.88 trillion miles (9.46 trillion kilometers)! One light-year is the distance light travels in one year. Astronomers measure the distance to a star as the number of years it takes the light from the star to reach us. We need a large unit like the light-year to make sense of the vast distances in space.

You will need:

a small rubber ball

an old stocking or long sock

1. Put the ball into the toe of the stocking.

2. Holding the end of the stocking, whirl the ball around your head. Do this outside in the open! Make sure no one is nearby!

Can you feel the ball trying to pull away? To keep it moving in a circle, you have to pull in the other direction.

This is how a planet travels around the sun. The planet is trying to escape, and the sun must pull on it to keep it in place. This pull is gravity. In the same way, the earth's gravity is the pull that keeps a satellite circling around it.

Going round in circles

3. Make sure no one is nearby and whirl the ball around again. What happens when you let go? The ball does not fly off in a circle.

It shoots away in a straight line. This is what would happen to a planet or satellite if the force of gravity suddenly stopped.

Rockets

If you want to travel into space, you can't fly there in a jet plane. Jet engines work by using oxygen from the air to burn their fuel. And, of course, there is no air in space. Fuel cannot burn without oxygen. The only kind of engine that will work in space today is the **rocket** engine. This is because it carries its own oxygen supply.

The Chinese invented the rocket about 800 years ago. They used gunpowder as fuel. Gunpowder is still used today in rockets that propel fireworks. They have a very simple design. The gunpowder is packed into a paper tube. When the rocket is lit, the powder burns. As it burns, the rocket gives out large amounts of hot gases. The gases come shooting out of the bottom end, pushing the rocket upwards in the opposite direction.

Some rockets use solid materials to propel, or push, them forward. These fuels are much more powerful than gunpowder, but they work in the same way.

Liquid-fuel motors

Most space rockets use liquid fuels. They are much more complicated than solid-fuel rockets. Most of the space inside the rocket is taken up by two storage tanks. One tank is for the fuel and one is for the **oxidizer,** the substance that provides the oxygen. The fuel and oxidizer are pumped into a **combustion,** or burning, chamber. There they are ignited. The hot gases produced shoot backwards out of the tail, and the rocket shoots forwards.

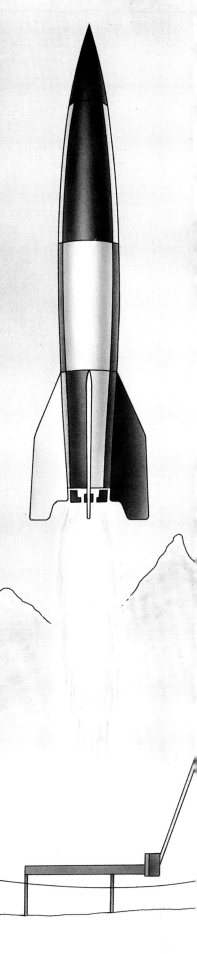

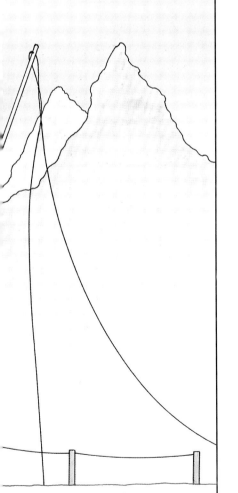

The V2 was a rocket-powered, guided missile used during World War II. V2's traveled faster than the speed of sound. Before they were launched, they could be programmed to hit a particular target.

Rocket fuel

It is best to do this experiment outside, as it makes a mess!

You will need:

a small plastic bottle

a cork

10 pencils

baking powder

a teaspoon

water

1. Place 10 pencils side by side, about 1 inch (2.5 centimeters) apart.

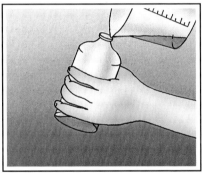

2. Put about five heaping teaspoons of baking powder into the bottle. Now add enough water in the bottle to cover the baking powder.

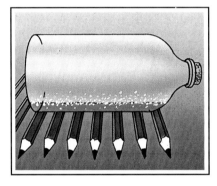

3. Quickly put the cork in and place the bottle on the pencils. Stand well back from one side of the bottle.

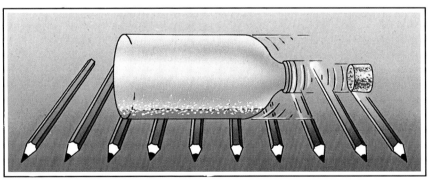

The baking powder and water start fizzing and making lots of gas. Pressure builds up inside and soon forces the cork out.

As the cork shoots out, the bottle shoots in the opposite direction over the pencils.

Step by step

One rocket by itself is not powerful enough to lift off into space. A series of rockets must be used. We call this combination a **multi-stage rocket.**

Most **launch vehicles** are multi-stage rockets with two or three separate rocket stages. The stages are usually joined together end to end. The first stage gives the ones above it a ride into space. After the first stage has run out of fuel, it falls away. The second stage takes over, using its own engines.

The tallest multi-stage rocket ever built was the American Saturn V rocket. It stood over 363 feet (110 meters) tall on the launch pad! It was made up of three stages.

The mighty Saturn V was built to launch the Apollo spacecraft to the moon in the 1960's and 1970's.

In the launching of a multi-stage rocket, the rockets fire one by one. Each falls away after its fuel has run out.

The Ariane 3 rocket takes off on a flight to launch communications satellites.

Rocket boosters

Some rockets have **boosters** attached to them. These fire to give the main rockets an extra boost at liftoff. Europe's Ariane rocket has boosters. So does the Russian Energia rocket, the most powerful rocket in the world.

36

Find out more by looking at
pages **30–31**
    38–40

Orbits

How far can you throw a ball? About 60 or 70 feet (18 or 21 meters)? Why doesn't it travel any farther? Gravity limits the distance. When you throw a ball, it rises into the air, but the earth's gravity soon pulls it back to the ground.

To launch a spacecraft, we somehow have to overcome gravity. How do we do this? We do it by speed. Think of yourself throwing the ball. If you throw the ball gently, it goes slowly, and it doesn't travel very far. But the harder you throw it, the faster it travels, and the farther it goes. You are starting to beat gravity by speed.

Falling forever

If you could throw the ball faster and faster, it would go farther and farther before it dropped back to the ground. Eventually, you could make it go so fast that its curve, as it fell, would be the same as the curve of the earth's surface. In other words, it would stay the same distance above the surface. It would then be in orbit around the earth.

Escaping gravity

To launch your ball into orbit you would have to give it a speed of more than 12 times that of a rifle bullet! The speed is over 17,000 miles (27,400 kilometers) an hour. This is known as the **orbital velocity.** If you wanted to send your ball to Mars or another planet, you would have to throw it even faster, at a speed of just over 24,800 miles (40,000 kilometers) an hour. Then it would escape earth's gravity completely. This speed is called the **escape velocity.**

In orbit

Space scientists send their satellites into orbit at orbital velocity. Up in space, about 186 miles (300 kilometers) above the earth, a satellite circles around the earth in about one hour. How does it stay circling up in space? Why doesn't it soon slow down and fall back to earth? The reason is that there is neither air nor anything else to cause **friction,** which would slow it down. So it circles round and round at the same speed.

Equatorial orbits go around the equator. Polar orbits go over the poles. In a geostationary orbit, a satellite keeps pace with the earth's rotation and appears fixed in the sky.

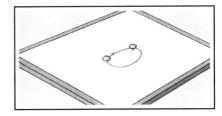

You will need:

a sheet of paper

a wooden board

a piece of string

a pencil

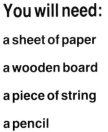

two thumbtacks

Draw an orbit

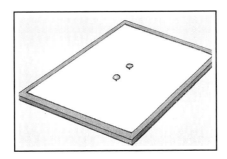

1. Place the sheet of paper on the board and stick in the two tacks about 4 to 5 inches (10 to 12.5 centimeters) apart.

2. Tie the ends of the string together and loop it around the tacks. The loop should be 1 or 2 inches (2.5 or 5 centimeters) longer than the distance between the tacks.

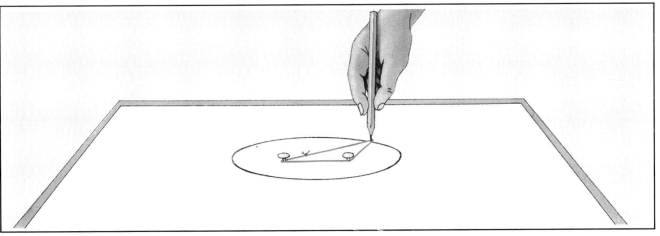

3. Place the pencil within the string as shown. Keeping the string tight, draw a line on the paper. Continue drawing all the way around the tacks.

You will find that you have drawn the shape of an oval. The proper name for it is an **ellipse.** Most satellites travel around the earth in an orbit that is an ellipse.

Change the size and shape of the ellipse by moving the tacks closer together or farther apart.

Find out more by looking at
pages **40–41**
      42–43

Satellite servants

In 1957, the first artificial satellite was successfully launched into orbit around the earth. Since then, more and more satellites have been launched into orbit. These satellites are helpful to people in many different ways. Communications satellites carry telephone calls and television programs between the earth's continents. Weather satellites help people to make accurate weather forecasts. Earth-survey satellites help people to make better maps and find where useful minerals are. And astronomers use satellites to study the universe.

Streamlined?

Satellites are built of lightweight materials. They are not streamlined, nor smooth like airplanes. Can you think why?

Engineers from the European Space Agency make final adjustments to an Olympus communications satellite.

Building a satellite

No matter what they are used for, most satellites have certain things in common. They carry a radio and several antennas. Some of the antennas are shaped like dishes. Satellites carry various measuring instruments and sometimes cameras. The radio sends, or **transmits,** the information back to Earth. On many satellites, there are large, flat parts that look like paddles. These are **solar cell** panels which capture the energy in sunlight and change it into electricity. The electricity powers the instruments and radio on board the satellite. Sometimes, the solar cells are fixed around the outside of the satellite.

Flash a signal

You will need:

a large balloon

string

silver paint

a flashlight

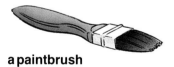

a paintbrush

This method of bouncing signals off a balloon was used to send the first radio messages through space in 1960. The balloon was called Echo I.

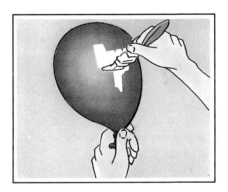

1. Blow up the balloon and tie the neck. Paint it all over with the silver paint, and let it dry.

2. Tie the thread to the neck of the balloon. Hang it outside, in a place where you and a friend can both see the same side of the balloon, but can't see each other. This could be in a doorway or on a tree.

3. In the dark, point the flashlight at the balloon and flash a coded message of short and long flashes. Your friend will see the flashes reflected, or bounced off, the balloon.

Communications and tracking

Scientists use radio to send signals to satellites and receive information from them. Satellites whizz endlessly around the earth. But you cannot send signals to a satellite if it is on the opposite side of the earth, because the earth blocks the signals.

Tracking

Before scientists can communicate with a satellite, they must know where it is. They must have a means of following, or **tracking,** it all the time. Again, they do this by radio. They use large dish antennas at tracking stations to listen for the satellite's signals. The antennas track the satellite's movement across the sky and exchange signals with it.

Find out more by looking at pages **36–37**

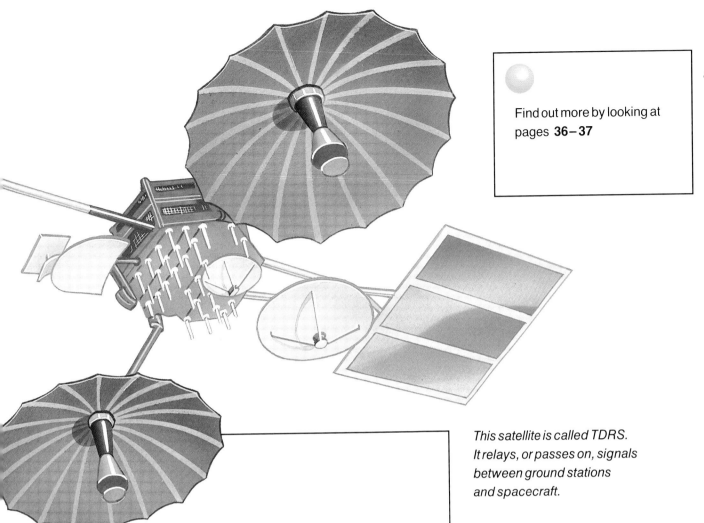

This satellite is called TDRS. It relays, or passes on, signals between ground stations and spacecraft.

Mission control

It is even more important for astronauts to keep in contact with the earth, so that the scientists on earth can check that everything is working properly on the spacecraft. The main communications center for manned trips in space is called **Mission Control.** The most famous Mission Control center is in Houston, Texas. The Russians have their communications center in Kaliningrad, on the Baltic coast.

Both the American and Russian communications centers use satellites and a network of tracking stations around the world. The American Mission Control uses a type of satellite called TDRS for communications. TDRS stands for Tracking and Data Relay Satellite. Astronauts and Mission Control communicate with each other by sending signals to each other via a TDRS.

42

Find out more by looking at pages **38–40**

Looking at the earth

It used to take a long time to make new maps of the earth. Teams of surveyors would work for years taking measurements of the earth over land and sea. Mapmakers needed many months to produce a map from these measurements.

Today, mapmaking is much easier because of satellites. From hundreds of miles up in space, satellites build up pictures of the land and sea in great detail. They show exactly what the land is like. They can also look at places where people cannot easily travel, such as high mountain ranges and the middle of deserts.

One of the best-known series of satellites used for surveying the earth is called the Landsat. Landsat satellites were built in the United States. France has built an earth-surveying satellite called SPOT. It also can send highly detailed pictures back to earth.

Invisible pictures

Survey satellites do not take photographs on film, like an ordinary camera. They take pictures in the same way as a TV camera. They make an image in the form of electronic signals and send the signals to earth. A computer changes the signals into an image on a screen or a photograph.

Survey satellites take pictures not only by using ordinary, visible light. They also take pictures using invisible rays, such as infrared. Infrared pictures show the temperatures on earth. They also can show whether areas are farmland or urbanized. The computer prints these in different colors.

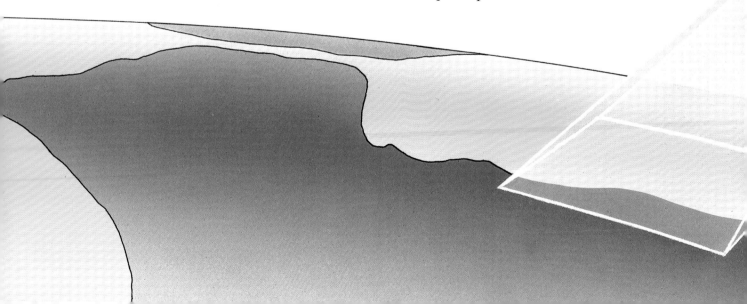

A satellite called Nimbus has shown that there is a hole in the ozone layer over the South Pole. This layer helps shield us from the rays of the sun that are harmful. Pollution is causing the ozone layer to break down. Nimbus helps scientists to monitor the hole in the ozone layer.

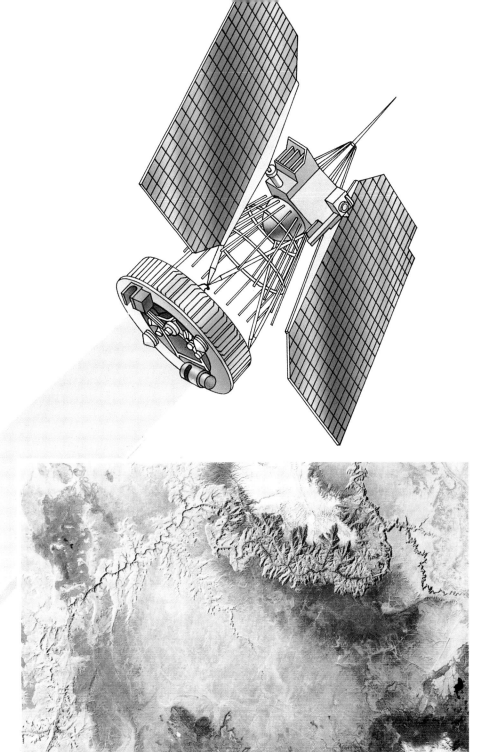

This is a photograph taken by U.S. survey satellite Landsat 1. It shows the Grand Canyon in Arizona.

Find out more by looking at pages **48–49**

Space traveling

Have you ever dreamed about traveling in space and going to the moon? Many people dreamed of space travel, even before the Space Age began. But it was not until April 1961 that a human being managed to travel in space. A Soviet pilot, Yuri Gagarin, was launched into a single orbit of the earth in a spacecraft called *Vostok 1*. Gagarin was the first cosmonaut. *Cosmonaut* is the Russian name for astronaut.

The first American in space was Alan Shepard. Shepard went 117 miles (188 kilometers) into space and came down again 15 minutes later. He did not go into orbit. Shepard's spacecraft was a small capsule called Freedom 7.

Life-support system

There is a great difference between a **manned spacecraft** and a satellite. A manned spacecraft must be able to carry human beings safely into space, keep them alive while they are there, and carry them safely back to earth.

To keep the crew alive, a manned spacecraft has a **life-support system.** This provides the astronauts with air, food, and water. It allows for breathing, eating, drinking, elimination of body wastes, sleeping, exercise, and recreation—all in a temperature-controlled environment.

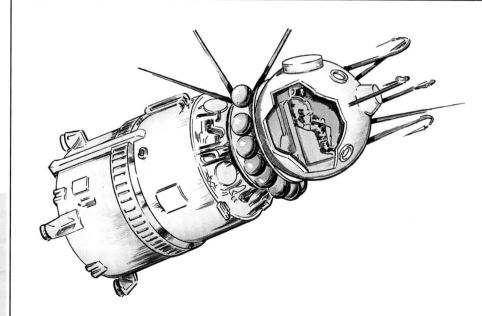

The first manned flight

This is the Vostok capsule in which Yuri Gagarin made the first manned flight in space on April 12, 1961. The capsule made a single orbit before returning to earth. The journey took 108 minutes.

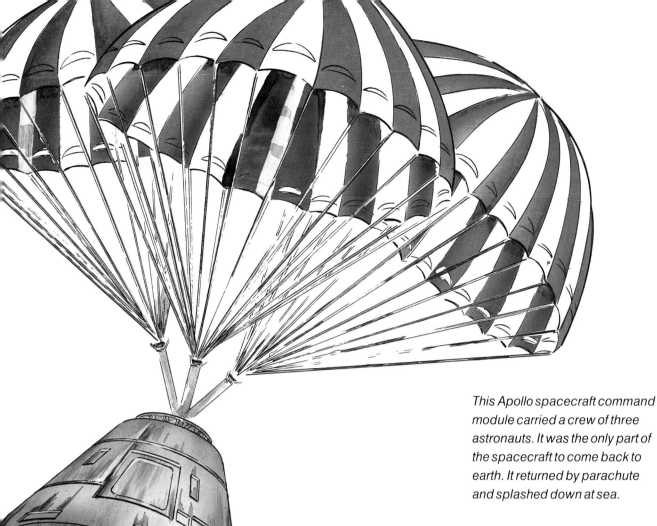

This Apollo spacecraft command module carried a crew of three astronauts. It was the only part of the spacecraft to come back to earth. It returned by parachute and splashed down at sea.

Re-entry

One of the most dangerous times for a crew of astronauts comes when their spacecraft returns to earth. It drops down from orbit, traveling at a speed of about 16,120 miles (26,000 kilometers) an hour. And it enters the earth's atmosphere at this speed. This return to the earth's atmosphere is called **re-entry.**

The air rubs against the outside of the spacecraft as it re-enters the atmosphere, making it slow down and heat up. The spacecraft is covered with a thick **heat shield.** If there were no shield, the spacecraft would burn up, just like a shooting star.

Space shuttle

Early spacecraft, such as Vostok and Apollo, were launched into space by huge rockets. Only the tiny capsule containing the crew came back, and that could never be used again. This was a very wasteful method of space travel.

In 1981, a new kind of spacecraft took to the skies. This space vehicle took off like a rocket and landed like an airplane. It first took off into space in April. By November, it was being used again — the first reusable, manned spacecraft. This craft was the American **space shuttle.**

The space shuttle launching system has three main parts. The crew flies in the **orbiter.** This looks rather like an ordinary plane with triangular wings. It flies into space mounted on a huge external **tank** which holds fuel for its engines. Just before a launch, two solid rocket boosters are fixed to the tank. They help to lift the shuttle high into the air, and then they fall away. The fuel tank falls away soon after. The orbiter is the only part which goes into orbit.

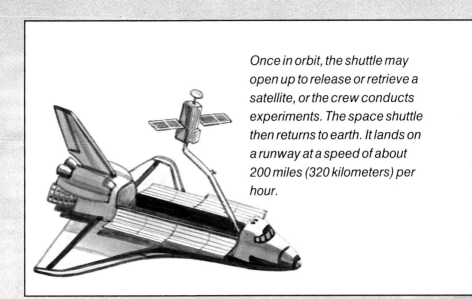

Once in orbit, the shuttle may open up to release or retrieve a satellite, or the crew conducts experiments. The space shuttle then returns to earth. It lands on a runway at a speed of about 200 miles (320 kilometers) per hour.

The space shuttle is the first reusable, manned spacecraft. It takes off using rocket boosters, which fall to earth by parachute when the fuel has been used up.

The orbiter

The orbiter has two main parts, a crew cabin in the nose and a huge bay behind for carrying **payload,** or cargo. The shuttle has carried satellites and space probes into space. The cargo bay has large doors that can open when the shuttle reaches orbit. The underside of the orbiter has a thick heat shield made up of more than 25,000 special tiles. This shield protects the orbiter when it re-enters the earth's atmosphere.

The crew cabin is supplied with air in the same way that an airliner is. The cabin has two main decks. The upper one is the flight deck, where the crew fly the craft. The front cockpit looks similar to that of an airliner, with more than 2,000 switches, buttons, and dials. The crew's living quarters are on the middeck underneath.

The United States has four orbiters in its shuttle fleet. These are *Atlantis, Columbia, Discovery,* and *Endeavour.* A fifth, *Challenger,* blew up during liftoff in 1986. Russia has a shuttle craft named *Buran.*

Find out more by looking at pages **50—51**

Effects of space travel

Imagine you are strapped into your seat in the space shuttle on the launch pad, ready for liftoff. The countdown comes to an end—"5. 4. 3. 2. 1. Ignition!" The rockets fire, and you feel yourself being pushed into your seat as the shuttle heads into the sky. The push you feel is called **G-force.** It makes your body feel up to three times heavier than usual. You can get an idea of what this feels like when you are in an elevator and it starts going up.

But when you get into orbit, the G-force stops. Suddenly, you feel you have no weight at all! You become weightless. We call this state **zero gravity,** or **zero g,** because it feels as if the earth's gravity, or pull, has gone. **Weightlessness** affects everything you do in space—walking, eating, drinking, and sleeping.

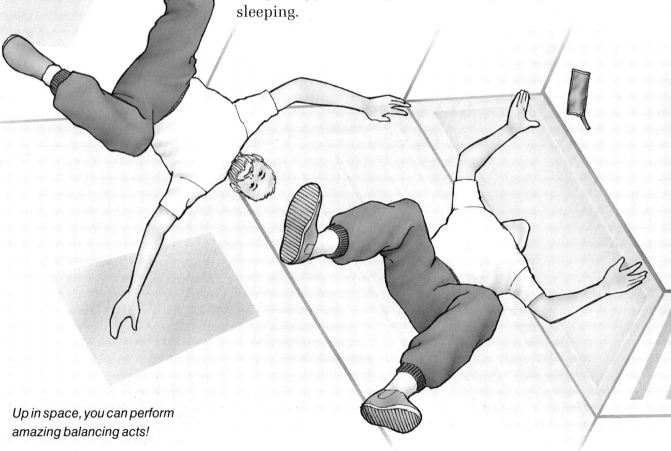

Up in space, you can perform amazing balancing acts!

Why can't you walk properly? Why isn't it a good idea to sprinkle pepper on your food? Why can't you pour yourself a drink? Why can't you sleep in an ordinary bed?

Space sickness

Up in orbit, it may be fun floating about and performing somersaults and other gymnastics. But your body isn't used to it, and you will probably feel sick. At least half of all astronauts suffer from **space sickness.** But after two or three days, your body gets used to the strange state, and the sickness stops.

On a long trip in space, weightlessness causes more serious problems. With no gravity to battle against, your muscles become weak and start to waste away. To prevent this, you must exercise regularly. On the shuttle, you can use a treadmill for exercise. On Russian space stations, the cosmonauts exercise on bikes that are fixed to the floor.

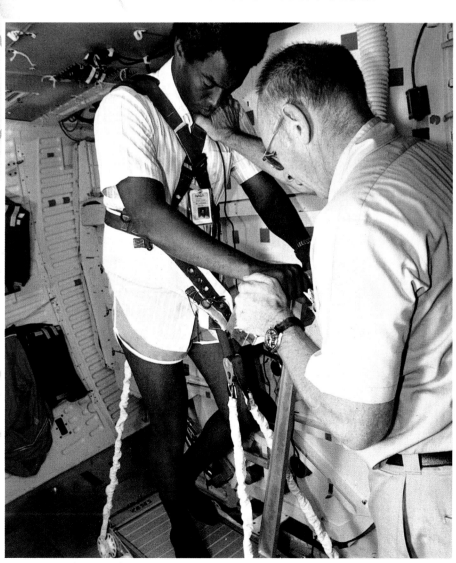

Astronauts have physical and medical checks before and after a space flight.

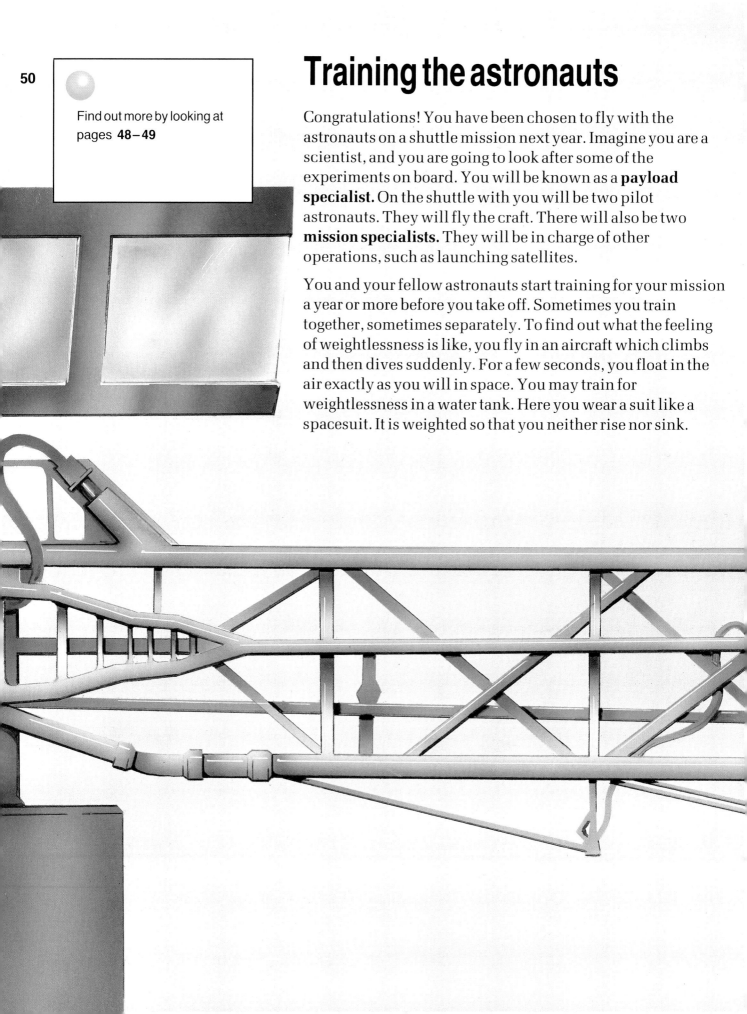

Find out more by looking at
pages **48 – 49**

Training the astronauts

Congratulations! You have been chosen to fly with the astronauts on a shuttle mission next year. Imagine you are a scientist, and you are going to look after some of the experiments on board. You will be known as a **payload specialist.** On the shuttle with you will be two pilot astronauts. They will fly the craft. There will also be two **mission specialists.** They will be in charge of other operations, such as launching satellites.

You and your fellow astronauts start training for your mission a year or more before you take off. Sometimes you train together, sometimes separately. To find out what the feeling of weightlessness is like, you fly in an aircraft which climbs and then dives suddenly. For a few seconds, you float in the air exactly as you will in space. You may train for weightlessness in a water tank. Here you wear a suit like a spacesuit. It is weighted so that you neither rise nor sink.

Like the real thing

You will also spend some time in a **simulator.** This is a dummy spacecraft, which looks like a real spacecraft inside. Here, you carry out rehearsals for liftoff and landing. The simulator has all the instruments of the real spacecraft. You even experience G-force. Through the windows of the simulator you see a view of the earth from space. The windows are actually video screens. The image is produced by a computer, which controls the whole machine. Flying the simulator is rather like playing a complicated video game.

During liftoff, astronauts experience G-force, which pins them down to their seats. They feel the same force when they train in a **centrifuge.** *This is a machine that whirls them around in an enclosed cabin at the end of a long arm.*

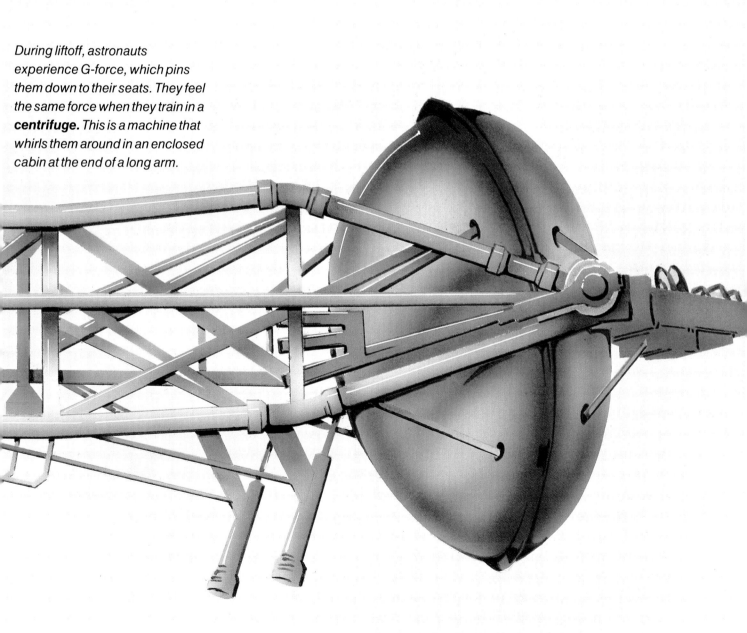

Spacewalking

Up in space, astronauts spend almost all the time inside their spacecraft. But sometimes the astronauts must go outside their craft to work. Going outside a spacecraft is called **extravehicular activity,** or EVA. The popular name for it is **spacewalking.**

The spacesuit

To protect them when they go spacewalking, the astronauts wear a special **spacesuit.** This gives them everything they need to stay alive. The suit is made of several layers. Oxygen for breathing is fed to an inner layer, which presses against the body. The outer layers protect the astronaut from flying particles. The white surface reflects sunlight.

Two astronauts flying in a ***manned maneuvering unit*** *(MMU) retrieve a satellite in space. They can move about in any direction by firing small jets fixed in different places on the machine.*

Inside, the astronaut is kept cool with water. Water flows through pipes in the astronaut's suit and carries away body heat. The cooling water is carried in a backpack, which is built into the top half of the spacesuit. This pack also holds the suit's oxygen supply, together with a radio and batteries.

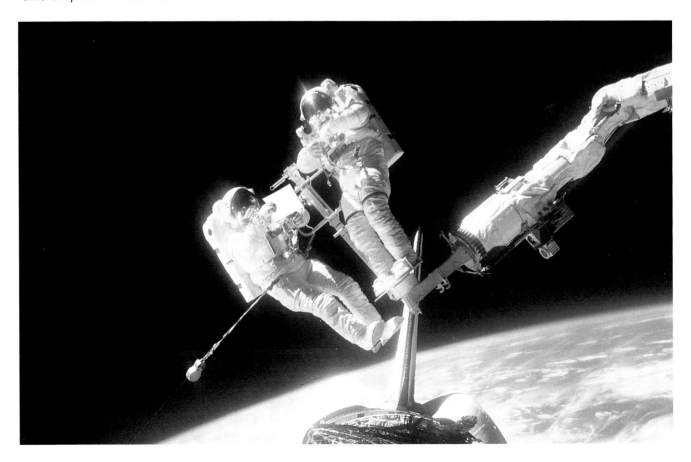

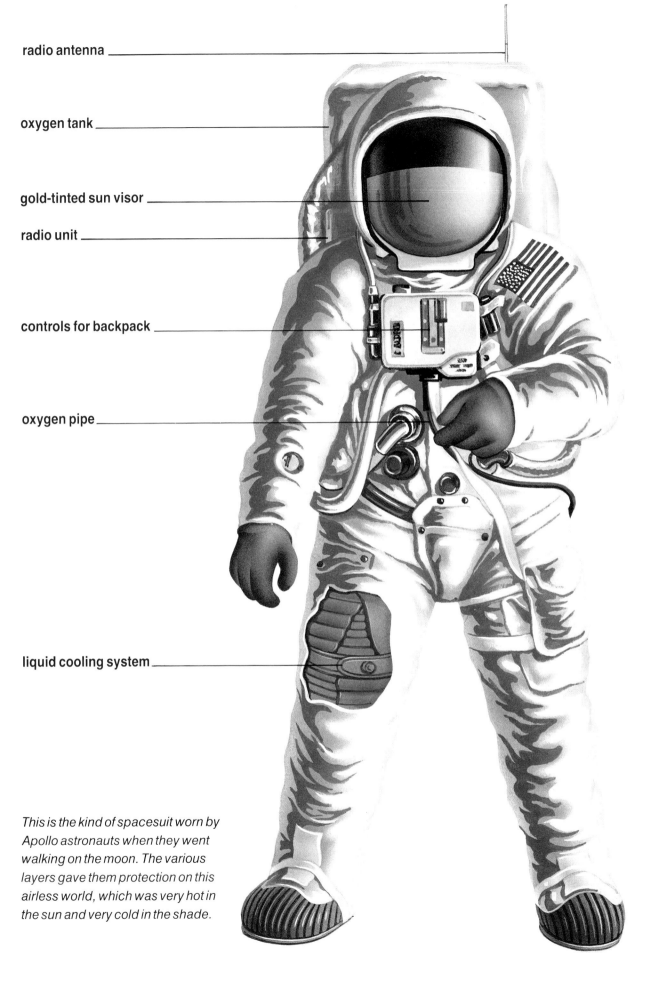

radio antenna

oxygen tank

gold-tinted sun visor

radio unit

controls for backpack

oxygen pipe

liquid cooling system

This is the kind of spacesuit worn by Apollo astronauts when they went walking on the moon. The various layers gave them protection on this airless world, which was very hot in the sun and very cold in the shade.

Space stations

Astronauts on the American space shuttle stay up in space for only about a week. But many Russian cosmonauts stay in space for months at a time. They live in a large spacecraft called a **space station,** which stays in orbit all the time. In 1987 and 1988, two Soviet cosmonauts, Vladimir Titov and Musa Manarov, spent a year in space.

Titov and Manarov stayed in the space station called *Mir.* Before Mir was put into orbit, the Soviets had launched seven *Salyut* space stations. The first one went into orbit in 1971. The last was *Salyut 7.* It is still in orbit, but no longer in use.

Mir and the Salyuts have similar designs. They are made in the shape of cylinders. They have two sets of solar panels to provide electricity. They carry all kinds of scientific instruments. The cosmonauts carry out experiments that require zero-gravity conditions. They also study the earth's surface and the universe. They keep a record of the effects of weightlessness on their bodies.

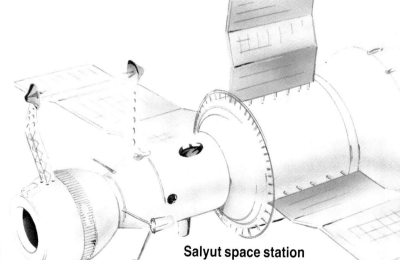

Salyut space station

A Soyuz spacecraft is joining, or **docking,** *with a Salyut space station. Russian cosmonauts use Soyuz to carry them up to their space stations.*

Soyuz spacecraft

The American space station Skylab should have looked like this in orbit. But one of the two big solar panels failed to open when orbit was reached. The astronauts used Apollo spacecraft to travel up to the station.

Skylab

American space scientists launched a space station called *Skylab* in 1973. Three teams of three astronauts visited the station and carried out different kinds of experiments and studies. These teams stayed, in turn, for 28, 60, and 84 days. At the time, they broke all records for staying in space. In 1979, however, the station fell from its orbit and broke apart. The United States has made plans to build a new space station, but progress has been slowed because of lack of funds.

Spacelab

Teams of scientists are also carried into space in the space shuttle. They work in a laboratory that fits into the shuttle's cargo bay. The laboratory is called *Spacelab 1*. It was built by the European Space Agency (ESA). Both American and European scientists carry out experiments in Spacelab. It stays in space for about a week at a time.

Find out more by looking at pages **12-13**

Going to the moon

The most exciting thing astronauts have done so far is to travel to the moon. They went in Apollo spacecraft, three astronauts at a time. Each Apollo spacecraft was made in three parts. The first part, the **command module,** carried the crew. The second, the **service module,** carried equipment and a rocket motor. The third, the **lunar module,** carried the astronauts down to the moon's surface. The spacecraft was launched by the mighty Saturn V rocket, the tallest rocket there has ever been. The journey to the moon took about three days.

The first astronauts landed on the moon on July 20, 1969, They were Neil Armstrong and Edwin Aldrin, from *Apollo 11*. Armstrong was the first person to set foot on the moon. As he stepped onto the moon, he said, "That's one small step for man, one giant leap for mankind."

Altogether, twelve astronauts from six Apollo spacecraft landed on the moon. They collected rocks, took photographs, and carried out experiments. The astronauts also set up scientific stations, which radioed their results back to earth. The stations carried on working long after the astronauts had returned to earth.

Landing on the moon

1. When an Apollo spacecraft was in orbit around the moon, two of the three astronauts climbed into the lunar module.

2. The lunar module separated.

3. As they approached the surface of the moon, they fired a rocket engine to act as a brake and landed gently.

4. When the lunar module took off again, it left behind its small launch pad.

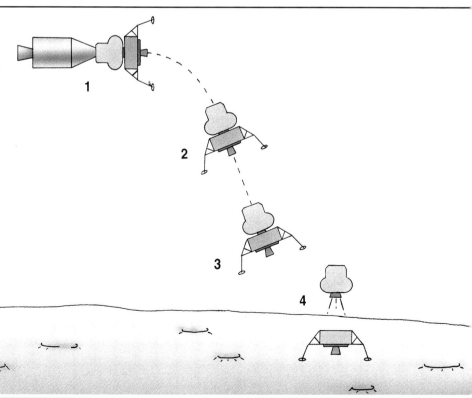

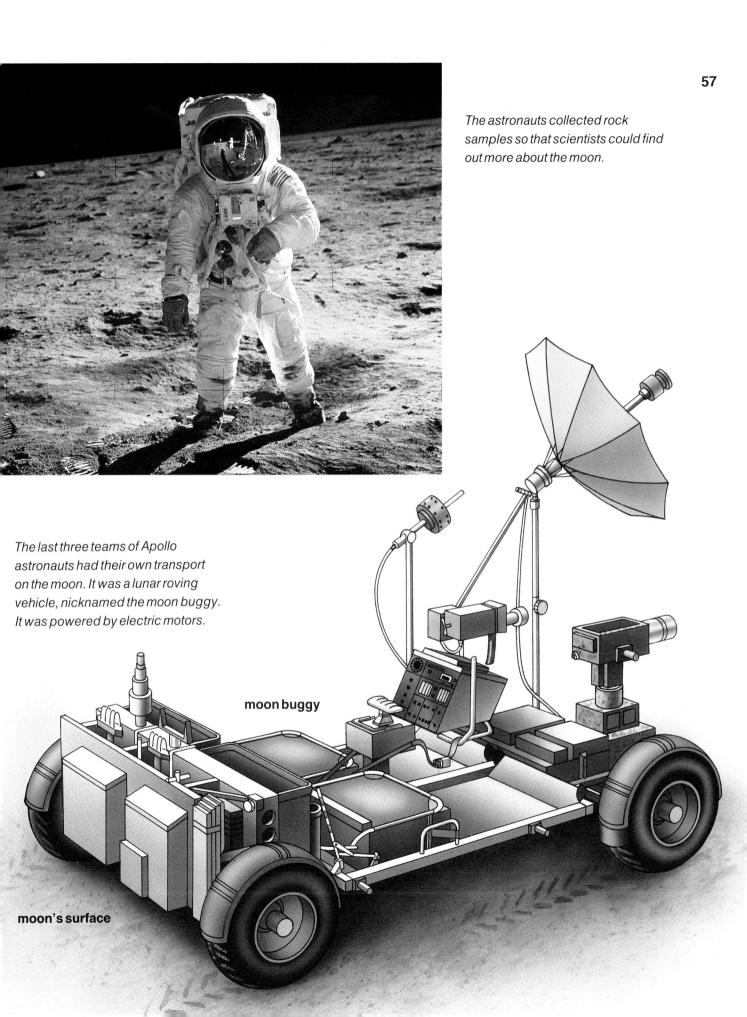

The astronauts collected rock samples so that scientists could find out more about the moon.

The last three teams of Apollo astronauts had their own transport on the moon. It was a lunar roving vehicle, nicknamed the moon buggy. It was powered by electric motors.

moon buggy

moon's surface

Space probes

Until now, human beings have traveled into space only as far as the moon, about 236,000 miles (380,000 kilometers) away. But they have sent robot spacecraft very much farther. These have visited the distant planets. The robot spacecraft are called **space probes.**

Space probes carry cameras and many kinds of instruments to study the planets they visit. They send information back to earth by radio. Probes must be launched from the earth at a very great speed — more than 24,800 miles (40,000 kilometers) an hour. Then they can escape from the earth's gravity. Aiming the probe is very difficult, because the planet it must reach is always moving. The probe must be aimed so that it reaches a point in space almost at the same time as its target. It must do this after a journey of many millions of miles, lasting for years.

This is the Mariner 10 probe that flew to Venus and Mercury in 1973 and 1974. It used solar cells for power because it flew close to the sun.

It is an astonishing fact that most probes sent to the planets have reached their targets. In 1989, the American probe *Voyager 2* flew past the planet Neptune almost exactly on time, after a 12-year journey. The planet was nearly 3.1 billion miles (5 billion kilometers) away from earth at the time. From this distance, the radio waves from *Voyager* took over four hours to reach the earth.

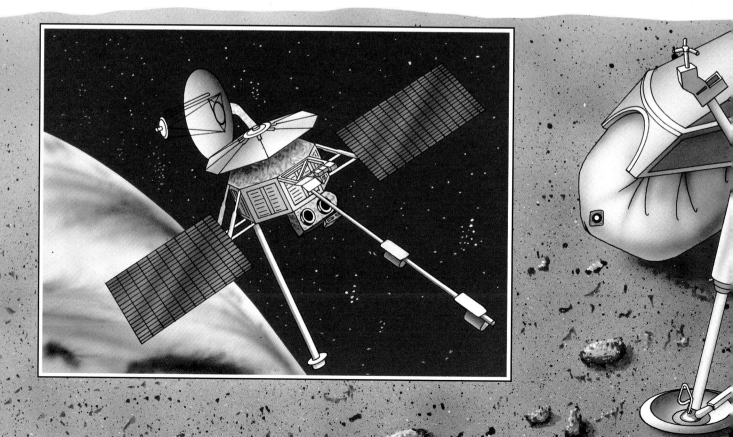

This illustration shows a Voyager probe photographing Uranus on the probe's journey into the outer solar system. The probe uses nuclear generators to make electricity. Solar cells can't be used because sunlight is too weak near Uranus.

Landers

Most probes study a planet as they fly past it. But some actually land on the planet and report back from its surface. A Russian probe, called *Venera*, was the first to land on a planet. It parachuted down to Venus in 1970. Since then, several Venera probes have sent back pictures of its surface. Two American Viking probes landed on Mars in 1976. They sent back pictures and reported on the Martian weather. They also examined the soil for signs of life—but didn't find any!

This is the Viking spacecraft that landed on Mars in 1976. It took close-up photographs of the landscape, dug into the ground, and tested soil in a miniature laboratory.

Voyage of discovery

On August 20, 1977, *Voyager 2* was launched into space. Two weeks later, *Voyager 1* set off. The two Voyagers are types of unmanned spacecraft called space probes. Their mission was to travel to the more distant planets of the solar system and send information about them back to earth. No spacecraft had ever traveled so far into space before.

Old-fashioned equipment

Voyagers 1 and *2* each carry 11 instruments. These include remote-controlled computers, television cameras, ray detectors, infrared and ultraviolet sensors, and a magnetometer. The instruments record and send back information about our solar system. Technology has developed quickly since the Voyager probes were launched. That equipment is now out of date. A modern, desktop computer is more powerful than the Voyager computers. Scientists have updated the probes' computer programs and made repairs from earth by remote control.

The journey of Voyager 2

1. On August 20, 1977, *Voyager 2* was launched from earth at a speed of just over 24,800 miles (40,000 kilometers) per hour. The idea was to use the gravity, or pull, of each planet it passed to catapult the space probe faster and faster through space, from one planet to the next.

sun

Earth

Jupiter

2. On July 9, 1979, *Voyager 2* came closest to Jupiter and discovered it has three more moons. The planet's gravitational pull increased the speed of *Voyager 2* to around 30,700 miles (48,000 kilometers) per hour.

3. It was August 25, 1981, and *Voyager 2* passed Saturn at a speed of 33,700 miles (54,400 kilometers) per hour. We learned that Saturn has nine more moons than it was known to have.

Saturn

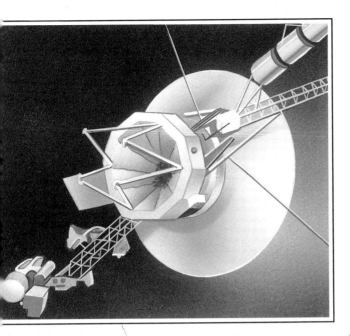

The space probe Voyager 2 traveled to two of the farthest planets in our solar system, Uranus and Neptune.

Voyager 2

Neptune

5. Mission completed! On August 25, 1989, *Voyager 2* passed within 3,000 miles (4,800 kilometers) of Neptune's cloud tops. We learned that this planet is a hostile world. No living thing could survive here.

4. At Uranus, on January 24, 1986, *Voyager 2* discovered 10 new moons. Its speed was now 36,700 miles (59,200 kilometers) per hour.

Uranus

Success for One ...

In 1980, three years after its launch, *Voyager 1* reached Titan, Saturn's largest moon. The probe sent back information to earth. It found chemicals like those on earth. But Titan is too cold for these chemicals to develop into living things as they have done on earth. *Voyager 1* is now heading out of the solar system towards deep, or **interstellar,** space.

... and for Two

Twelve years after it left Earth, *Voyager 2* reached Neptune. It had traveled nearly 4.4 billion miles (7.1 billion kilometers) and arrived four minutes early! The probe's instruments should work for another 25 years. So the next messages may come to us from deep space.

Both *Voyager 1* and *Voyager 2* carry a message—a record of voices and other sounds from earth—just in case there is life beyond our solar system.

Glossary

Asteroid belt:
Thousands of rocky bodies circling the sun in a band between Mars and Jupiter.

Atmosphere:
Layer of gases around a planet.

Black hole:
Small area of space with so much gravity that not even light escapes.

Comet:
Lump of ice and dust, with gas tail, that travels through solar system.

Constellation:
Pattern of stars, such as the Dipper.

Crater:
Hole on surface of a planet or moon caused by rocks falling from space.

Escape velocity:
Speed required to lift an object completely out of the earth's gravity.

Galaxy:
Group, or cluster, of millions of stars, such as the Milky Way Galaxy.

Gravity:
Attraction, or pull, between two objects. It becomes stronger as their mass increases and weaker as the distance between them increases.

Launch vehicle:
Multistage rocket and its payload, or cargo.

Life-support system:
System of supplies and controls that keeps humans alive in space.

Light-year:
Distance that light travels in one year, or 5.88 trillion miles (9.46 trillion kilometers).

Meteor:
Piece of rock from space that enters the earth's atmosphere and burns up.

Meteorite:
Meteor that does not burn up completely, but strikes the earth.

Multistage rocket:
Series of rockets in which each one pushes those above it higher and falls off when its fuel is spent.

Nebula:
Great cloud of gas and dust floating in space. Stars form inside *nebulae.*

Neutron star:
Tiny star made up of particles called *neutrons,* left from a *supernova.*

Observatory:
Building that houses a telescope.

Orbit:
The path of a smaller heavenly body around a larger one.

Orbital velocity:
Speed required to lift an object into orbit around the earth.

Phases of moon:
Changing shapes of the moon caused by its reflecting sunlight as it moves around the earth.

Planet:
One of nine bodies circling the sun.

Radio telescope:
Telescope that uses radio waves sent out from a star to study the star.

Ring:
One of the bands of rocks and ice that orbit some planets.

Rocket engine:
Engine carrying its own oxygen supply.

Solar cell panel:
Panel that changes the energy of sunlight into electricity.

Solar system:
The sun and its planets, their moons, the asteroids, comets, and meteors.

Space probe:
Type of robot spacecraft that investigates far-distant space.

Space shuttle:
Type of reusable, manned spacecraft.

Space station:
Type of manned spacecraft that stays in orbit for extended lengths of time.

Supernova:
Explosion of a star.

Telescope:
A device for seeing far. Telescopes that depend on light use lenses.

Index